GOD IS ENERGY. DO YOU BELIEVE?

...The Higher Being...

Book 2

by Semisi Pule

Copyright © Rainbow Enterprises 2014

Publisher: Rainbow Enterprises 2014

ISBN: 978-1-927308-11-0

All rights reserved. No part of this book shall be reproduced in any way without prior written permission from the publisher and copyright holder. Rainbow Enterprises is the trade/publisher name of Semisi Pule also known as (aka) Semisi Pule Pone.

Email: rainbowenterprises7@gmail.com, semisipone@yahoo.com

"Great spirits have always encountered violent opposition from mediocre minds. The mediocre mind is incapable of understanding the man who refuse to bow blindly to conventional prejudices and chooses instead to express his opinions courageously and honestly".

Albert Einstein, 1940. Wikiquotes.

CONTENTS.

Introduction....5

1. The Beginning....13

2. The Mind....22

3. Notes on the main Religions....29

4. Enlightenment....47

5. The Promised Kingdom....52

6. Concluding Comments...57

Literature Cited...60

Introduction.

This book is the second in this series on "creation and science". It is an attempt to collect existing information to explain our existence on earth. We cannot be an accident of nature. An evolutionary mutation in space and time which manifests itself in flesh and blood.

It is not a new idea. It is as old as time itself. The Higher Being is part of the Cosmic Spirit according to Hindu belief, for example. So this book will put together some ideas supported by literature to clarify exactly how the body works in relation to its true form, the cosmic self, the spirit, the Higher Being.

When I was at the University of Auckland, one of my Professors....John Morton...who was a "zoologist", always mention "evolution in the bible" during his invertebrate lectures. He was a man who spent years studying small animals on the beaches and reefs. He said something to the effect....that **"they are so perfect and beautiful, they cannot be an accident of nature....it must be evolution in the biblical sense".** I think it means that evolution was inspired by divine beings. A creation that has no beginning or end. All living organisms evolving all the time into a better form.

That got me interested in the topic of "creation and science". What if.... science can be used to explain the spiritual world? The only problem, of course, is that we use "brick and mortar" analysis to analyse what cannot be seen. We have seen numerous TV documentaries trying to take photos of ghosts. We know ghosts are spirits, they are invisible to the naked eye. We cannot take photos of them!

Like the atoms or energy, we know spirits exist because we can sometimes see the "effect" but cannot see them. In the same TV documentaries looking for ghosts, gadgets that measure energy in the air can sometimes detect the "presence" of "something"......an energy being in the air..... but it cannot be photographed. They cannot see it. Only the energy meter can "see it". Just like a current meter detecting the presence of an electric current.

Energy is invisible to the human eye. We cannot take photos of energy. We can see its effects like light bulbs turned on by electricity, trees moved by the wind, planes flying in the air, humans running around, vehicles moving on the road and so on. The light and movements are caused by some form of energy, but we cannot see the energy itself.

Science has already explained the presence of energy. We know it exists. The total amount of energy in the universe is the same all the time. We cannot destroy it or create any more, but we can change it from one form into another. From solar energy into mechanical energy or heat energy and so on. Energy stored in petrol can be used to move vehicles, ships and planes. Energy stored in food can be used to move humans and living organisms. Energy stored in uranium can be exploded to do a lot of damage or harnessed to create electricity and mechanical energy.

Much of this was discussed in the first book **"God is Energy. Do you Believe? "**. Man also changes from one form into another. From "flesh and blood" into a "spirit being". Man is made up of energy. The bible say that man was made in God's image. According to Hindus, when the body of flesh and blood dies the "spirit being" goes back to the "Cosmic Spirit".....in my view the totality of the energy in the Universe. This is probably the heaven that Christians talk about, being one with God. Muslims call it paradise. Buddhists, on the other hand, think achieving nirvana or "enlightenment" and escaping samsara or the endless cycle of births, deaths and rebirths driven by karma, is the goal of human existence. Perhaps they too join the cosmic spirit after being liberated from the sufferings of reincarnation?

Einstein did point out that mass is made of energy and therefore the whole universe is made up of energy. We can safely conclude, that if God belongs in our universe, it must be made of energy. In that sense, the Cosmic Spirit is the total amount of energy in the universe, God.

In the Bible, when Jesus ascended to heaven he sent the Holy Spirit to empower the apostles. The Holy Spirit came like "the roar of a great wind" which looks like "tongues of fire". It entered the apostles and they were able to speak in other languages and perform miracles.

Modern man is also able to perform miracles in the name of science. In the last book, **"God is Energy. Do you Believe?"** I concluded that the Holy Spirit must be the driver of all these miracles.

An attempt will also be made....in this book.... to explain how man develops with the "evolution of the spirit". Man's body is like a car. It cannot move by itself. It needs a driver. Man can drive a car, but he needs to learn how to drive and also gain experience to become a good driver. Similarly, our bodies cannot move by itself, it needs the "spirit" to drive it. We can tell how the spirit evolves throughout the life of the "man", as a baby, child, young adult and wise old man.

Would you rather that the Holy Spirit is your driver? If the Evil One is your driver you will find out quickly that he does not waste time. You will have so much trouble that your only solution is to run to God.

Throughout this book, I would like you to think of the meaning of these verses from the bible...

Luke 24:49-51

(Luke's version is similar to St John's).

"I am going to send you what my father has promised; but stay in the city until you have been clothed with the power from on high.

When he had led them out to the vicinity of Bethany, he lifted up his hands and blessed them and was taken up into heaven."

St Mark records it differently.

Mark 16 : 15-18

He said to them, "Go into all the world and preach the good news to all creation. Whoever believes and is baptized will be saved, but whoever does not believe will be condemned. And these signs will accompany those who believe; In my name they will drive out demons; they will speak in new tongues; they will pickup snakes with their hands; when they drink deadly poison it will not hurt them at all; they will place their hands on sick people and they will get well".

The promise of receiving the Holy Spirit and believing in Jesus Christ gives man the power to perform miracles in his name.

Acts 2: 1-4

"When the day of Pentecost came, they were all together in one place. Suddenly a sound like the blowing of a violent wind came from heaven and filled the whole house where they were sitting. They saw what seemed to be tongues of fire that separated and came to rest on each of them. All of them were filled with the Holy Spirit and began to speak in other tongues as the Spirit enabled them".

In the last book "**God is Energy. Do you Believe**?" I discussed "man the miracle maker" because Jesus had sent him the Holy Spirit which helped him to perform miracles....or "speak in other tongues".

The Holy Spirit is still with us to-day helping us to "raise the dead", "change water into wine", "walk on water" and so on. We have our own miracles to add to the ones in the bible....flying machines, computers, electricity and so on.

Hopefully, at the end of this book we have "connected the dots" between "man the flesh and blood" and "man the spirit"....an analysis of a spiritual kind....finding evidence of....The Higher Being, The Cosmic Spirit.

Enjoy.

Chapters 1.   The Beginning

When the male sperm enters the female egg, it passes its information and "fuses" with the egg to become a "fertilized egg" which began dividing furiously into an embryo. The embryo has begun to develop legs, arms, a torso and head. As it gets bigger, it became more and more complex with inner organs, brains, blood vessels, nerves and so on. Finally, in the ninth month when the baby is complete; it is born into the world as a separate person from its mother. Sometime between fertilization and being born, it learned or acquired the ability to exist by itself without being connected to its mother all the time.

Since birth the baby learns to eat, drink, laugh, make noises and speak, walk, run and play. At the age of 3, the toddler starts kindergarden and learns to sing, dance and socialize with other kids. Then he/she goes to Primary School, Intermediate School, High School then University where he/she is taught everything he/she needs to know to be a "successful adult".

It is interesting to note that although the spirit is in the child, yet the child still behaves like a child. If the spirit is born together with an infant surely the child will show the wisdom of the spirit or "The Higher Being" from an early age. The explanation, I believe, lies in the "car analogy"....the child's body. You can only do certain tasks with a car. A truck can carry a heavier load. A crane does different tasks. It is possible that the spirit, although it is the guide and mentor, can only do what is possible to the child. Therefore, if you are in a car, you cannot carry 100 people like a train. You can only perform like a car. This is a simplistic explanation but one that clearly demonstrates the point. A child can only do things that are possible to her/him at the particular age.

Furthermore, a child will have to learn to speak, to read and write and even to think logically. From an early age, parents can tell whether the child is normal or not.

Sometimes a child does not develop normally. There have been writers who point out that this abnormality is the affliction of the spirit not the body. In certain religions, it is called "karma" or the result of your previous sins. So it is the manifestation of the spirits "state of health" that is exhibited in the child. The symptoms are signs that all is not well with the spirit.

> **Karma** - In Indian tradition, the principle that a person's actions have consequences that merit reward or punishment. Karma is the moral law of cause and effect by which the sum of a person's actions are carried forward from one life to the next, leading to an improvement or deterioration in that persons fate.
>
> **Penguin Encyclopedia.**

When the spirit leaves the body, the body "dies". Eyes of dead people are opaque and show no life in it. You can tell the eyes of a dead person from a live one simply by looking at it. It is lifeless, it does not have the "spark" in the eyes of the living. In addition, the body cannot move by itself. A dead body is lifeless, no matter what age it is. How does the spirit make the body move? And why does it decide to leave a body?

> Most Hindus believe that the spirit or soul – is the true "self" of every person, called the atman — is eternal.
>
> Hinduism. Wikipedia.

In my previous book "**God is Energy. Do you Believe?**", the energy from the sun and its flow through the food chain is discussed. There is also discussion of the "Energy Being" or Higher Being and its relation to energy. Einstein's equation $E = mc^2$ gives us a clue to this phenomenon. It means that the energy in a body is equal to its mass multiplied by the square of the velocity of light. Therefore, small amounts of mass can release large amounts of energy and large amounts of energy are required to create a small amount of mass. It follows, therefore, that mass and energy is one and the same thing. **The only conclusion we can draw is that the whole of the universe is made up of energy. God is Energy.**

> "It follows from the special theory of relativity that mass and energy are both but different manifestations of the same thing.....a somewhat unfamiliar conception for the average mind. Furthermore, the equation $E = mc^2$, in which energy is put equal to mass, multiplied by the square of the velocity of light, showed that very small amounts of mass may be converted into a very large amount of energy and vice versa".
>
> Albert Einstein, Theory of Relativity. Wikiquotes.
>
> (this theory was demonstrated experimentally by Cockcroft and Walton in 1932).

I have already discussed in **"God is Energy. Do you Believe"** that the spirit or Energy Being is part and parcel of God. The Higher Being is God. And God is the Universe because everything is made up of God himself or energy. Mass and Energy is one and the same thing. The atom bomb is proof that $E = mc^2$ works. A small amount of mass or radioactive metal can release a huge destructive amount of energy. Two atomic bombs were dropped on Hiroshima and Nagasaki in Japan, during World War II, by the Americans, caused so much terrible destruction that the Emperor and army of Japan surrendered immediately. Einstein was part of the team that worked to develop the atom bomb. It is called the atom bomb because the idea is to split the atoms of the radioactive fuel to release the energy stored in it. So much energy is released, all at once, that it has a huge amount of destructive power.

> **Mass and Energy are one and the same thing. It follows that everything in the universe is energy. It is part and parcel of God.**

This why the spirit can move the body because the spirit or God is energy. The energy that man uses came from the sun, trapped in the chloroplast of plants and stored in carbohydrate and nutrients in plants that man eats as rice, bread, vegetables and fruits to get his energy source. However, without the spirit it cannot use that energy source because the body would be lifeless. Is not God, the Spirit, the giver of life according to the scriptures?

So what is the point of being born and grow into an adult? Then die and decompose? To be eaten by smaller animals and microbes? To live and learn subjects at school, find a job, start a family, save some money, buy a house and build up one's wealth when the only sure reward on earth is death? And you cannot take anything with you to the next life.....except perhaps your karma.

You may also ask...what is the point of building cars and developing the technology to build and release better cars every year? Of building and developing all the other machinery and gadgets that man uses while he lives on earth? If the only sure way for it is the rubbish dump? Or being recycled into other goods?

I think the analogy makes sense.

Here's what Hinduism say about it;

This cycle of action, reaction, birth, death and rebirth is a continuum called samsara. The notion of reincarnation and karma is a strong premise in Hindu thought. The Bhagavad Gita states:

As a person puts on new clothes and discards old and torn clothes, similarly an embodied soul enters new material bodies, leaving the old bodies.

Wikipedia.

Evidence of the spirit also surface in the hospitals where "clinical death" patients talk about "floating in the air"!.

> **"When a person dies in the hospital....Doctors are able to revive him by passing an electric current through his heart. But is it his heart they are restarting? Or they are simply "reviving the energy being within?".**

There are many stories of clinical death in the hospitals. Of patients who have died for a few minutes...and they say that they have a sensation of looking down on their bodies as if they are floating in the air like a ghost! They watch the Doctors trying to revive them and....suddenly they wake up like they were asleep! Does the electric current attract the "spirit" back into the body with the energy boost?

It may be worth studying such phenomenon as it is a "window" into the spirit world. Man might find out a lot more about his "inner self" or spirit.

Chapter 2. The Mind

The Mind is also referred to as the "Inner Self" and many other names. But if we look at the human body and all the functions of its different parts....the only conclusion is that the mind must be in the brain. It is the thinking and intuitive part of the brain. It "knows" a lot of things without even reading or studying the subject. Could it be that the "Inner Self" is "The Higher Being" himself ?. Giving you instructions and information that you need when you have not heard or seen it before? You just have a hunch that it could be right? Or you feel that it is the right one?

When you talk or do things, it is recorded in your brain. You can recall the particular event and conversation that took place many years later. Most people remember them for life. What does that information do? Does the "brain" or "inner self" use it unconsciously to help you? Is that intuition or imagination? A total recollection and use of your memory?

The memory does help you with your very survival. You avoid fires because you know it is hot. You don't jump off high buildings because you know you will get injured. You remember to eat and drink, wash yourself and do many other things to ensure your survival.

> "I believe in intuition and inspiration....at times I feel certain I am right while not knowing the reason. Imagination is more important than knowledge. For knowledge is limited, whereas imagination embraces the entire world, stimulating progress, giving birth to evolution. It is, strictly speaking, a real factor in scientific research."
>
> Albert Einstein, 1931. Wikiquotes.

In learning and scientific research your brain uses the information stored to make conclusions and ask questions that ultimately give you the answers you are looking for. Does that mean your body and its parts are intelligent?

We all accept that the genes contain all the necessary information for the development of new life from male and female parents. But where does the genes get its information. How tall, hair, skin and eye colour, intelligence and so on? Can it be that our words and thoughts stored in the brain are used to write the genetic code into our genes? Can we influence the future generations through our words and deeds by writing what we want into the genetic code? A book can influence human kind for generations. The bible is one example. Do genes work in the same way?

> "You shall not make for yourself an idol in the form of anything in heaven above or of the earth beneath or in the waters below. You shall not bow down to them or worship them...for I, the Lord your God, am a jealous God, punishing the children for the sins of the fathers to the third and fourth generation of those who hate me, but showing love to a thousand generations, of those who love me and keep my commandments".
>
> Commandment 2, Ten Commandments; Exodus 20 : 4.

The 2nd commandment in the Ten Commandments of Moses...given by God....suggest that God punish people for up to the 3rd and 4th generations....of those who "hate him"....and pray to other idols as Gods. Does this suggest "genetic coding"....that the words and deeds of the fathers will lead to their children's misfortunes? Or perhaps God strike them down with a bolt or lightning? Or endless cycles of rebirth....bad karma?

When the words and deeds are recorded in the brain, they can be recalled in a lifetime. If told to others or passed down as oral genealogy, they can be remembered for several generations. People do take action on these stories. But what about the brain or inner self? Is this karma?

> Karma translates literally as action, work, or deed, and can be described as the "moral law of cause and effect". According to Hindu literature an individual develops "impressions" from actions, whether physical or mental. A body more subtle than the physical one but less subtle than the soul, retains impressions, carrying them over into the next life, establishing a unique trajectory for the individual.
>
> Hinduism, Wikipedia.

It seems that Hinduism believe that "impressions" developed from "actions"....probably spoken words or thoughts....are carried into the next generation and do influence the new babies being born. This information is not written in the genetic code...so where is it stored? It must be in the parent and passed to the offspring through the genes.

I once worked as a Salesman and one of the "success methods" we were taught is the power of affirmations. We were taught to write down what we want to happen in our sales presentation and recite it 100 times before making the presentation. I can say that it gave me a lot of confidence and conviction about my presentation. I can feel that my potential buyer is also convinced by my presentation, because through the affirmations, I convinced myself.

The same thing happens with Evangelists. They pray and prepare themselves for their sermon. I have heard some whose words were so powerful many people were converted. Some of the converts were crying and confessing their sins to God. Evangelists are well known for praying for "assistance" from God before they give their sermon. Does God give power ....through affirmations and prayer?".....to empower one to convert the listeners?   Jesus did say......"ask and you shall receive".

The "inner self" must be the mechanism of control here. It records and act upon the words or the prayers. It is possible that the new cells produced in the body everyday are influenced in this way that their genetic makeup include the thoughts and words of that individual. Have you ever heard relatives say..."your grandson speaks and behaves like his father or grandfather?"....

This means that the genetic material passed on from the father is expressed in the kid's behaviour. But how did that genetic information got written into the genes in the first place? We all know it is a chemical process but we also know that feelings, words and thoughts do influence the production of chemicals in the body. Feelings of happiness or anger influences what chemicals the body produce. This maybe how we influence our genetic makeup. And this is probably what God refers to as his vengeance ....down to the third and fourth generations. The sins and deeds of the fathers are passed on in their genes to the children. It may cause sickness, paralysis and other disabilities. Karma of a very serious nature.

> "The ultimate goal of life, referred to as moksha, nirvana or samadhi, is understood in several different ways: as the realization of one's union with God; as the realization of one's eternal relationship with God; realization of the unity of all existence; perfect unselfishness and knowledge of the Self; as the attainment of perfect mental peace; and as detachment from worldly desires. Such realization liberates one from samsara and ends the cycle of rebirth. Due to belief in the indestructibility of the soul, death is deemed insignificant with respect to the cosmic self. Thence, a person who has no desire or ambition left and no responsibilities remaining in life or one affected by a terminal disease may embrace death".
>
> Hinduism. Wikipedia.

Chapter 3. Notes on the main Religions.

I will briefly comment and display "summarized" information, from Wikipedia, on each of the major religions in this chapter to compare the similarities or differences in achieving the "state" of being "enlightened" and escaping suffering....returning to God or the Cosmic Spirit as believed by most of the major religions.

Hinduism is the oldest religion on earth. It is a complex culture of "dharma" or ethics and duties, "samsara" or the continuing cycle of birth, life, death and rebirth driven by "karma". The soul or spirit is eternal unless one wish to liberate oneself from samsara by abandoning all human desires or moksha....and return to the Cosmic Spirit.

Yoga is referred to as the right path. There are millions of people around the world who practice "yoga".

HINDUISM

"Hindus do not appear to have any differences with any other religion, welcoming all religions. Hinduism is not just a faith. It is the union of reason and intuition that cannot be defined, but is only to be experienced. Hinduism's tolerance to variations in belief and its broad range of traditions make it difficult to define as a religion according to traditional Western conceptions.

Unlike other religions in the World, the Hindu religion does not claim any one Prophet, it does not worship any one God, it does not believe in any one philosophic concept, it does not follow any one act of religious rites or performances; in fact, it does not satisfy the traditional features of a religion or creed. It is a way of life and nothing more.

Also, Hinduism does not have a single system of *salvation*, but consists of various religions and forms of religiosity. Some Hindu religious traditions regard particular rituals as essential for salvation, but a variety of views on this co-exist. Some Hindu philosophies postulate a theistic ontology of creation, of sustenance, and of the destruction of the universe, yet some Hindus are atheists, they view Hinduism more as philosophy than religion. Hinduism is sometimes characterised by a belief in reincarnation (samsara) determined by the law of karma and the idea that *salvation is freedom from this cycle of repeated birth and death*. Hinduism is therefore viewed as the most complex of all the living, historical world religions".

Hinduism, Wikipedia.

In Christianity it is the acceptance or belief in Christ who died on the cross to save the world from sin. John 3:16 gave this promise...."That whoever believeth in him shall not perish but have eternal life". It appears that there is a similarity that death is followed by being "born again" or rising from the dead. Eternal life can be "returning to the Cosmic Spirit or God" which is eternal.

"Hindu practices generally involve seeking awareness of God and sometimes also seeking blessings from deities. Therefore, Hinduism has developed numerous practices meant to help one think of divinity in the midst of everyday life. *Mantras* are invocations, praise and prayers that through their meaning, sound, and chanting style help a devotee focus the mind on holy thoughts or express devotion to God/the deities.

Many devotees perform morning ablutions at the bank of a sacred river while chanting.

Hinduism grants absolute and complete freedom of belief and worship. Hinduism conceives the whole world as a single family that defies the one truth, and therefore it accepts all forms of beliefs and dismisses labels of distinct religions which would imply a division of identity. Hence, Hinduism is devoid of the concepts of apostasy, heresy and blasphemy.

Samsara provides ephemeral pleasures, which lead people to desire rebirth so as to enjoy the pleasures of a perishable body. However, escaping the world of samsara through moksha is believed to ensure lasting happiness and peace. It is thought that after several reincarnations, an *atman* eventually seeks unity with the *cosmic spirit.*"

Hinduism is based on "the accumulated treasury of spiritual laws discovered by different persons in different times". The scriptures were transmitted orally in verse form to aid memorization, for many centuries before they were written down. Over many centuries, sages refined the teachings and expanded the canon. In post-Vedic and current Hindu belief, most Hindu scriptures are not typically interpreted literally. More importance is attached to the ethics and metaphorical meanings derived from them. Most sacred texts are in Sanskrit".

Hinduism, Wikipedia.

The following is a summary of the Buddhist idea of how man will find peace and escape reincarnation and sufferings of the flesh on earth.

BUDDHISM

"Buddhism is a nontheistic religion that encompasses a variety of traditions, beliefs and practices largely based on teachings attributed to Siddhartha Gautama, *who is commonly known as the Buddha, meaning "the awakened one".* According to Buddhist tradition, the Buddha lived and taught in the eastern part of the Indian subcontinent sometime between the 6th and 4th centuries BCE. He is recognized by Buddhists as an awakened or enlightened teacher who shared his insights to help sentient beings end their suffering through the *elimination of ignorance* and craving *by way of understanding* and with the ultimate goal of attainment of the sublime state of *Nirvana".*

Buddhism, Wikipedia.

> **Buddhism, unlike Christianity and Hinduism, aim to eliminate ignorance through understanding and achieving "Nirvana" or "Awakening" or "Enlightenment"; thus escaping samsara...the cycle of births and rebirths. Perhaps through "abandoning all worldly desires".**

Buddhism is practiced primarily in Asia, estimates of Buddhists worldwide vary significantly depending on the way Buddhist adherence is defined. Estimates range from 350 million to 1.6 billion, with 350–550 million the most widely accepted figure. Figures for Christianity could be as high as 2-3 billion and 1.5-2 billion for Hindus. Moslems also have about 1-2 billion members.

"Buddhist schools vary on the exact nature of the path to liberation, the importance and canonicity of various teachings and scriptures, and especially their respective practices. The foundations of Buddhist tradition and practice are the Three Jewels: the Buddha, the Dharma

(the teachings), and the Sangha (the community). Taking "refuge in the triple gem" has traditionally been a declaration and commitment to being on the Buddhist path, and in general distinguishes a Buddhist from a non-Buddhist

The evidence of the early texts suggests that Siddhārtha Gautama was born in a community that was on the periphery, both geographically and culturally, of the northeastern Indian subcontinent in the 5th century BCE. After the birth of young prince Gautama, an astrologer named Asita visited the young prince's father—King Śuddhodana—and prophesied that Siddhartha would either become a great king or renounce the material world to become a holy man, depending on whether he saw what life was like outside the palace walls. Śuddhodana was determined to see his son become a king, so he prevented him from leaving the palace grounds. But at age 29, despite his father's efforts, Gautama ventured beyond the palace several times. In a series of encounters—known in Buddhist literature as the four sights—he learned of the suffering of ordinary people, encountering an old man, a sick man, a corpse and, finally, an ascetic holy man, apparently content and at peace with the world. These experiences prompted Gautama to abandon royal life and take up a spiritual quest.

Gautama first went to study with famous religious teachers of the day, and mastered the meditative attainments they taught. But he found that they did not provide a permanent end to suffering, so he devoted himself to meditation, through which he discovered what Buddhists call the Middle Way, a path of moderation between the extremes of self-indulgence and self-mortification.

Gautama was now determined to complete his spiritual quest. At the age of 35, he famously sat in meditation under a sacred fig tree — known as the Bodhi tree — in the town of Bodh Gaya, India, and vowed not to rise before achieving enlightenment. After many days, he finally destroyed the fetters of his mind, thereby liberating himself from the cycle of suffering and rebirth, and arose as a fully enlightened being . Soon thereafter, he attracted a band of followers and instituted a monastic order. Now, as the Buddha, he spent the rest of his life teaching the path of awakening he had discovered, travelling throughout the northeastern part of the Indian subcontinent, and died at the age of 80 (483 BCE) in Kushinagar, India".

Buddhism, Wikipedia.

Within Buddhism, samsara is defined as the continual repetitive cycle of birth and death that arises from ordinary being's grasping and fixation on the self and experiences. Specifically, samsara refers to the process of cycling through one rebirth after another within the six realms of existence,[a] where each realm can be understood as physical realm or a psychological state characterized by a particular type of suffering. Samsara arises out of ignorance and is characterized by suffering, anxiety and dissatisfaction.

Karma - In Buddhism karma is the force that drives samsara—the cycle of suffering and rebirth for each being. Good, skillful deeds and bad, unskillful actions produce "seeds" in the mind that come to fruition either in this life or in a subsequent rebirth. The avoidance of unwholesome actions and the cultivation of positive actions is called "ethical conduct". In Buddhism, karma specifically refers to those actions of body, speech or mind that spring from mental intent and bring about a consequence or fruit, or result.

Buddhism, Wikipedia.

Some karma "maybe just part of the universe" and similar to forgiveness of sin, negative karma, can be "forgiven" through recitation of special scriptures....or prayers. Negative karma is said to cause the cycle of suffering which results from births, deaths and rebirths. Escaping samsara is the ultimate "salvation"....which is similar to Hinduism.

"Rebirth refers to a process whereby beings go through a succession of lifetimes as one of many possible forms of sentient life, each running from conception to death. *Buddhism rejects the concepts of a permanent self or an unchanging, eternal soul, as it is called in Hinduism and Christianity.* According to Buddhism there ultimately is no such thing as a self independent from the rest of the universe. Buddhists also refer to themselves as the believers of the "anatta" doctrine. Rebirth in subsequent existences must be understood as the continuation of a dynamic, ever-changing process of "dependent arising", determined by the laws of cause and effect (karma) rather than that of one being, transmigrating or incarnating from one existence to the next".

The Buddha's teachings is based on the Four Noble Truths, regarded as central to the teachings of Buddhism, and are said to provide a conceptual framework for Buddhist thought. These four truths explain the nature of suffering, anxiety, unfulfilled, its causes, and how it can be overcome. The four truths are:

1. The truth of suffering, anxiety, being unfulfilled (dukkha).

2. The truth of their origin

3. The truth of their cessation

4. The truth of the path leading to their cessation

The obvious suffering of physical and mental illness, growing old, and dying. The anxiety or stress of trying to hold onto things that are constantly changing. A subtle dissatisfaction pervading all forms of life, due to the fact that all forms of life are changing, impermanent and without any inner core or substance. On this level, the term indicates a lack of satisfaction, a sense that things never measure up to our expectations or standards.

The second truth is that the origin of dukkha can be explained as craving conditioned by ignorance. On a deeper level, the root cause of dukkha is identified as ignorance of the true nature of things. The third noble truth is that the complete cessation of dukkha is possible, and the fourth noble truth identifies a path to this cessation.

Nirvana

Nirvana means "cessation", "extinction" of craving and ignorance and therefore suffering and the cycle of involuntary rebirths (samsara), "extinguished", "quieted", "calmed"; it is also known as "Awakening" or "Enlightenment" in the West. The term for anybody who has achieved nirvana, including the Buddha, is arahant.

Awakening of arahants is more commonly translated into English as "enlightenment", a meaning synonymous to nirvana, using only some different metaphors to describe the experience, which implies the extinction of greed, craving, hate, aversion and delusion.

The Mahayana tradition separated them and considered that nirvana referred only to the elimination of craving (passion and hatred), with the resultant escape from the cycle of rebirth. This interpretation ignores the third fire, delusion: the extinction of delusion is of course in the early texts identical with what can be positively expressed as gnosis, Enlightenment.

Buddhas

According to Buddhist traditions a Buddha is a fully awakened being who has completely purified his mind of the three poisons of desire, aversion and ignorance. A Buddha is no longer bound by Samsara and has ended the suffering which unawakened people experience in life. Therefore, Siddhartha Gautama was not the only Buddha. The history shows a list of 28 Buddhas and also many Buddhas of celestial, rather than historical, origin.

Buddhism, Wikipedia

The following is a summary of the "essence" of the religion of Islam. It is slightly different in that emphasis is on the "resurrection of the body" rather than "rebirth" of the spirit. However, the Muslims believe that, after death, they will "enter" paradise if they live life according to the teachings of the prophet Muhammad.

ISLAM

"Islam is a monotheistic and Abrahamic religion articulated by *the Quran (Koran), considered by its adherents to be the word of God (Allah)* **and** *by the teachings and normative example of Muhammad , considered by them to be the last prophet of God.* **An adherent of Islam is called a**

Muslim. Muslims believe that God is one and incomparable and *the purpose of existence is to worship God.* Muslims also believe that *Islam is the complete and universal version of a faith that was revealed before many times throughout the world, including through Adam, Noah, Abraham, Moses and Jesus, whom they consider prophets.*They maintain that the previous messages and revelations have been partially misinterpreted or altered over time, but consider the Arabic Quran to be both the unaltered and the final revelation of God. Religious concepts and practices include the five pillars of Islam.... They are (1) the shahadah (creed), (2) daily prayers (salat), (3) almsgiving (zakah), (4) fasting during Ramadan and (5) the pilgrimage to Mecca (hajj) at least once in a lifetime. Islam believers demonstrate submission to God by serving God, following his commands, and rejecting polytheism. *Muslims and Jews repudiate the Christian doctrine of the Trinity and divinity of Jesus, comparing it to polytheism.* In Islam, God is beyond all comprehension and Muslims are not expected to visualize God, the most common Allah..."The Compassionate" or "The Merciful". Allah is the term with no plural or gender used by Muslims and Arabic-speaking Christians and Jews to refer to God".

Islam, Wikipedia.

The Quran, and the Islamic holy books are the records which most Muslims believe were dictated by God to various prophets. *The Quran is divided into 114 chapters, which combined, contain 6,236 verses.* The chronological order are primarily concerned with ethical and spiritual topics. Muslims identify the prophets of Islam as those humans chosen by God to be his messengers. The Quran mentions the names of numerous figures considered prophets in Islam, including Adam, Noah, Abraham, Moses and Jesus, among others. Muslims believe that God finally sent Muhammad as the last prophet to convey the divine message to the whole world.

Similar to Christianity and Hinduism , Muslims believe in the **"judgement and day of resurrection"**. They belicve the time is preordained by God but unknown to man, but the emphasis is on a bodily resurrection...not a spiritual one....

"Ritual prayers must be performed five times a day. The prayers are done with the chest in direction of Mecca though in the early days of

Islam, they were done in direction of Jerusalem. A mosque is a place of worship for Muslims. "Zakāt" is giving a fixed portion of accumulated wealth by those who can afford it to help the poor or needy and for those employed to collect Zakat. Fasting, from food and drink (among other things) must be performed from dawn to dusk during the month of Ramadhan. The pilgrimage, called the ḥajj has to be done during the Islamic month of Dhu al-Hijjah in the city of Mecca. Every able-bodied Muslim who can afford it must make the pilgrimage to Mecca at least once in his or her lifetime, following the foot steps of Abraham..... recounting the steps of Abraham's wife, while she was looking for water for her son Ismael in the desert before Mecca developed into a settlement".

Islam, Wikipedia.

A Brief History of Islam

In Muslim tradition, Muhammad (c. 570 – June 8, 632) is viewed as the last in a series of prophets. During the last 22 years of his life, beginning at age 40 in 610 CE, according to the earliest surviving biographies, Muhammad reported revelations that he believed to be from God conveyed to him through the archangel Gabriel (Jibril). The content of these revelations, known as the Quran, was memorized and recorded by his companions.

During this time, Muhammad in Mecca preached to the people, imploring them to abandon polytheism and to worship one God. Although some converted to Islam, Muhammad and his followers were persecuted by the leading Meccan authorities. The Arab tribes in the rest of Arabia then formed a confederation and during the Battle of the Trench besieged Medina intent on finishing off Islam. Muhammad was victorious in the nearly bloodless Conquest of Mecca, and by the time of his death in 632 (at the age of 62) he united the tribes of Arabia into a single religious polity.

The largest denomination in Islam is Sunni Islam, which makes up 75%–90% of all Muslims. While the Sunnis believe that a Caliph should be elected by the community, rejecting the legitimacy of the previous Muslim caliphs. Shia Islam has several branches. There are also other smaller groups. Sufism is a mystical-ascetic approach to Islam that seeks to find divine love and knowledge through direct personal experience of God. By focusing on the more spiritual aspects of religion, Sufis strive to obtain direct experience of God by making use of "intuitive and emotional faculties" that one must be trained to use.

A comprehensive 2009 demographic study of 232 countries and territories reported that 23% of the global population, or 1.57 billion people, are Muslims. Of those, it is estimated over 75–90% are Sunni and 10–20% are Shia with a small minority belonging to other sects. Approximately 57 countries are Muslim-majority, and Arabs account for around 20% of all Muslims worldwide.

The majority of Muslims live in Asia and Africa. Approximately 62% of the world's Muslims live in Asia, with over 683 million adherents in Indonesia, Pakistan, India, and Bangladesh. In the Middle East, non-Arab countries such as Turkey and Iran are the largest Muslim-majority countries; in Africa, Egypt and Nigeria have the most populous Muslim communities. Most estimates indicate that the People's Republic of China has approximately 20 to 30 million Muslims.

Islam, Wikipedia.

Chapter 4. Enlightenment

> "The Compact Oxford Dictionary describes "Enlightenment" as "the gaining of knowledge and understanding". It was also a movement in Europe in the 17th and 18th century emphasizing reason and individualism rather than tradition".

Enlightenment can be achieved through study of the scriptures or attaining of knowledge through school and research. Buddhist monks spent a lifetime studying the old teachings and practicing meditation. In order to reach that higher goal of becoming all wise and knowing the "right path", one must achieve the state of nirvana or being "awakened" or "enlightened".

Many religious people also practice and study their old scriptures to gain enlightenment. In the Christian bible, Luke 24 :44-47 talks about *Jesus opening the disciples eyes* so that they can understand what has been written about him in the scriptures. The disciples reached the state of being "enlightened" when Jesus opened their eyes. They understand what has been written in the Law of Moses and by the prophets and in the Psalms.

Luke 24 : 44-47.

"This is what I told you while I was still with you. Everything must be fulfilled that was written about me in the Laws of Moses, the prophets and the Psalms. Then he opened their minds so they could understand the Scriptures. He told them, "This is what is written: The Christ will suffer and will rise from the dead on the third day, and repentance and forgiveness of sin will be preached in his name to all nations, beginning at Jerusalem.

It appears that enlightenment is a state of mind. Jesus simply "*opened their minds*" so they can understand the scriptures" and he also sent the Holy Spirit to change them from ordinary men into Super Beings. They were able to "heal the sick and drive out demons in the name of the Lord".

Jesus, from all accounts, was the "enlightened one" the "Super Being" or "The

Higher Being" that we all should be....but we need to be "awakened".

In Mark 6 : 49 - 50

"But when they saw him walking on the lake, they thought he was a ghost. They cried out because they all saw him and were terrified".

In St Matthews account....St Peter asked Jesus if he can walk on the water too, *but he sank as soon as he took a few steps on the water*. He did not have enough faith to hold him up in the water. He began worrying about sinking rather than "doing the walking"....that Jesus commanded him to do. *This is the difference between an awakened being and one that is not. An awakened being can walk on water.*

This is the problem with becoming enlightened, man does not have the "power of faith" to hold him up in the water. He knows that he cannot walk on the water. Even though a man will claim he has great faith....still he knows he cannot walk on water. It is only the power of the Holy Spirit that will allow him to walk on water, heal the sick and drive out demons. The Holy Spirit allows him to become a "Super Being" by bringing out the power of the "inner self"..."The Higher Being" that is present in all of us.....*by being "awakened" like the Buddha. Enlightened.*

Study does give a man a certain amount of knowledge. Einstein suggested that a man also needs imagination, intuition and fantasy in order to become enlightened. To reach that higher goal of knowledge that can only be achieved when "God opens ones eyes to know what is hidden" from all mortals. We can refer to Einstein as an "enlightened man". He was able to find the truth about energy or what God wants him to find. **A discovery so great that Albert Einstein is revered by all scholars and people who know of his work.** He is among the immortals like Mahommed, Buddha and the Gods.

Science has many more "universal truths" that man has uncovered. Man has become a miracle maker, through the power of the

Holy Spirit. Any man can turn water into wine by adding alcohol and flavours, any man can walk on water using technology, doctors heal the sick and raise the dead.

We know that since the Holy Spirit came "like the roar of a great wind" and took over the apostles....who became "awakened" or "enlightened". They spoke in other languages and performed miracles.

Through the promise of the Holy Spirit, anyone who believes in Jesus Christ becomes "awakened". They are the miracle makers of to-day, the 20th century. But the revelations made by the Holy Spirit is so far reaching that education can also "awaken" mankind. God has chosen to enlighten mankind if they choose to embrace it. Just like his miracles that come from the life giving sunshine and the rain.

God does not choose who receives life giving sunshine and water....it is a gift for all of mankind. Just like being enlightened by education.

Chapter 5. The Promised Kingdom

Science sometimes talks about parallel universes that exist together with ours. Any of those parallel universes could be the paradise often talked about in the religions of the world. There are certain "gates" that we go through to enter. There can be unlimited numbers of parallel universes, but like Einstein say that even though his positive knowledge was great....he truly values his ability to fantazise...it was a great tool in his scientific research, being able to imagine the solution.

There is a story about St Peter being the "Gate Keeper" into the Kingdom of Heaven...and it is entirely possible it is a kind of parallel universe.

The whole of the Christian faith is the promise made by Jesus **in John 3:16..."That God so loved the world that he gave his only begotten son....that whoever believeth in him shall not perish**

but have everlasting life". Most Christians believe that this refers to the soul. It is man's soul or spirit that will live forever. Not his human form of flesh and blood. Again, we encounter the idea of "The Higher Being". To have everlasting life and live forever, it only means that the soul, spirit or the "Higher Being" is a super being capable of powers beyond human comprehension.

In the book of **Acts 2: 1-4** the Holy Spirit became one with the apostles;

"When the day of Pentecost came, they were all together in one place. Suddenly a sound like the blowing of a violent wind came from heaven and filled the whole house where they were sitting. They saw what seemed to be tongues of fire that separated and came to rest on each of them. All of them were filled with the Holy Spirit and began to speak in other tongues as the Spirit enabled them".

And they were able to perform miracles in the name of Jesus. Consider the case of the cripple outside the temple gates. Peter and John were entering the temple and a crippled man asks them for money.

Acts 3: 1-8.

One day Peter and John were going up to the temple at the time of prayer...at 3 in the afternoon. Now a man crippled from birth was being carried to the temple gate called Beautiful, where he was put everyday to beg from those going into the temple courts. When he saw Peter and John about to enter, he asked them for money. Peter looked straight at him as did John. Peter said, "Look at us!". So the man gave them his attention, expecting to get something from them.

Then Peter said, "Silver or gold I do not have, but what I have I will give you. In the name of Jesus Christ of Nazareth, walk". Taking him by the right hand, he helped him up, and instantly the man's feet and angles became strong . He jumped to his feet and began to walk.

What the cripple got was far more precious than a silver or gold coin. God through the Holy Spirit and St Peter gave him his freedom. His ability to walk again. There were many other miracles performed by the apostles in the name of Jesus....with the help of the Holy Spirit.

All the major religions have one goal in common. *"Man returning to the Cosmic Spirit"* as the Hindus put it. The Cosmic Spirit is the essence of God...and I say...the energy driving the universe. It appears that the promised Kingdom is God himself. God is the Universe...but is it this one or a parallel one? But then God is all powerful and all encompassing that anything is possible.

When every person dies, all major religions agree they will return back to God; whether they are punished through karma and samsara as the Hindus and Buddhists believe or return in their human body is irrelevant. I think we all agree that God is the Cosmic Spirit, the Universe and he is all knowing and all powerful.

Jesus did say that when Christians are "born again" and accept him as their saviour he becomes one with them. He lives his life through them. They become *"one with GOD"*. It is very similar to returning to the Cosmic Spirit as believed by Hindus. They are saved and will enter the promised kingdom....perhaps the Cosmic Kingdom! The Kingdom of Heaven, a parallel universe.

Anything is possible.

The Cosmic self is eternal. It has no beginning or end. *Hindus belief that the Cosmic self is the "true-self"*....the human body being just a punishment....demoted to the endless cycle of birth, death and rebirth until one finds redemption through Christ, nirvana or liberation from karma.

CHAPTER 6. CONCLUDING COMMENTS

The bible refers to "eternal death" or what Jesus call "condemnation". It is becoming clear that it means the total and complete loss of man "the flesh and blood". Only man "the spirit" will survive. When man "the flesh and blood" dies he returns to the cosmic spirit according to Hinduism; or it ascends to heaven according to Christians. Only the Muslims believe that man "the flesh and blood" will arise from the dead, a gift from Allah to believers of the prophet Muhammad.

The marriage of science and creation has created some interesting questions but it also demonstrates that the world is "interconnected". The material and the spiritual world are mutually inclusive. *Scientists call them "parallel universes".* You can enter these parallel universes through "gates". Do all religions have their own parallel universe? Can the "collective mind" create a new "parallel universe"?.

The Christian religion talks about St Peter as the "Gate Keeper"...and Jesus did say that

"Peter is the rock" and on that rock he will build his church. Is St Peter the gate keeper to the parallel universe we go to when we die? Heaven?

Einstein was thankful for his ability to fantasize because it enabled him to "imagine the solutions" to the hard Scientific questions he faced. The discovery of $E = mc^2$ is a discovery so great it does lend good reason to the use of fantasy or imagination to solving "impossible" problems....scientific or not.

There are clues to the existence of "The Higher Being" in us all. The Spirit. Sometimes it is the unconscious mind that gives us the answers. People often speak of things they are not aware or know of. Simply a "slip of the tongue", but if you think about it; nothing you do is accidental. It is all controlled by your "mind"...The Higher Being.

In the Christian belief, being "born again" is accepting Jesus Christ died on the cross to save the world and forgive their sins. When you accept Jesus as your saviour he will enter your body and become you. He will live your life for you. This is God's way of bringing you back to him. Returning to the Cosmic spirit ....in Hinduism.

It is becoming clear *"that man cannot live by bread alone"*. Man needs the spirit or he will die. When the **Higher Being** leaves him his body becomes lifeless and "returns to the earth where it came from".

Literature Cited....

1. The Holy Bible - Authorized King James Version

2. The Holy Bible - New International Version

3. Penguin Encyclopedia

4. Compact Oxford Dictionary

5. Wikiquotes - Internet Free Encyclopedia

6. Wikipedia - Internet Free Encyclopedia.

www.ingramcontent.com/pod-product-compliance
Lightning Source LLC
Chambersburg PA
CBHW061252040426
42444CB00010B/2365